Mixing Up the Medicine

A Collection of Poems

Antonino Monti

NFB
<<◇>>
Buffalo, NY

Copyright © 2015 Antonino Monti

Printed in the United States of America

Monti, Antonino

Mixing Up the Medicine/ Monti- 1st Edition

ISBN: 978-0692405635

1. Mixing Up the Medicine – Poetry– Verse.
No Frills.
Title

No part of this book may be reproduced or transmitted in any form by any means, electronic or mechanical, including photocopying, recording, or by any information storage and retrieval system without permission in writing by the author.

No Frills Buffalo
119 Dorchester Buffalo, New York 14213
For more information visit
Nofrillsbuffalo.com

I would like to dedicate this book to the City of Syracuse.

Contents

I. Mixing Up the Medicine

Dream of a Tree	10
The Glory	12
The Lights	14
Dream	16
Settle In	19
My Papa's Gone Whaling	20
A Mission of Falling	21
Time	22
Pink Dreams	23
The Sun Doesn't Lie	25
Mixing Up the Medicine	26
Ride the Snake	29
Hear the Moon Call	30
Climb Aboard the Train	32
The Lonely Mountain	33
Anonymous	35
Tomorrow	37
The Island	39
The Being Returns	41
Lead Me	42
Dear Lord	44
The Veil of Existence	46
Be a Friend	47
My Friend	48
Chariot Ride	49
The Saber	50
Lost in a Sea of Frustration	51
She is Crying	53
An Undiscovered Goddess	54
The Marching Band	55
A Quest for Endless Glory	56

A Veil of Innocence	58
In the Pig Pen	59
In an Endless Game	60
Remove Oppression	61
Bears Dance with the Elves	62
Your Magic Aura of Alcoholic Funk	64
Crawl	65
We Have Won	66
Reality Has Become Digital	67
Does it Make Sense?	69

II. Your Cute Little Nose Inspires Poetry and Prose

I Stand Alone	72
The Wrong Side of the River	74
Elizabeth	75
The Embers	77
No Direction	78
Only the Brute	79
Love Notes: Volume One	81
With a Careless Glare	83
Golden Runes	84
I Fly Nocturnal	85
It Started at Birth	87
Ivy Eyes	88
Your Golden Locks	89
Aimless Verse From 83'	90
Says the Dark Queen	91
Lioness of My Dreams	92
Your Voice isn't Choice	93
The King's Flowers	94
The Horizon of Lost Souls	95
Sierra	96
Our Endless Night Crawl	98
My Queen Be	99

I Decree to Thee	100
It's All a Dream	101

III. Hear the Call Above It All

Out of Bounds	104
An Old Oak Tree	106
The Observer	107
Mankind's Only Secret	108
Reflections of Our Meager Existence	110
Sex Over All	111
A World Without My Pen	112
The American High	113
We are Cult Followers	114
Half Thoughts	115
We Owe it All to the Sun	116
Fingertip Picking	117
No Mercy	118
The Prison is Calling Me	119
Watchmen	120
A Life That Contains More	121
The Answer is on the Ground	122
The Demon	123
Technicolor Boxes	124
The Trees of Our Forefathers	125
Victims of the Circumstance	126
Bar Strategy	127
Someone to Blame	128
Are We the Teenager?	129
A Little Game They Call Life	130
Drunken Chronicles	131
An Over Beaten Cow	132
For Too Long She Has Sat Dormant	133
Blue Flame	134

IV. Ascending into Asgard

The Call	136
Runic Translations	137
Princess of the Daunting Waters	139
Galloping to the Gallows	140
Hail to the Stars,	
Those Who Set the Bar	141
A Man in Moss	143
In the Pig Pen	144
The Blues Saloon	145
Cambodia	147
I Was a Fool Made Wise	148
Our Invitation	150
In the End	151
The Black Arrow	152
The Internet is a Religion	153
Victory in Valhalla	154

I
Mixing Up the Medicine

Dream of a Tree

It's as if the world falls into place
giant blocks falling from the sky
forming a perfect wall.
The wall expands on to eternity
only to arrive at the beginning,
angels descend down to bless the creation
only to be trapped by the dragon,
Trojan horse.

Another day begins
and you are tall
reaching out into the sky.
The burning ball of energy
warms the air
and you feel it on your skin.
Breath
in and out,
relax
there's no need for alarm.
Creaking in the distance
someone is coming,
sharp axe in hand.
No! No!
What are you doing?
Chop chop
he hacks away at your knees
but you turn the other cheek,
they know not of what they do.
Finally in one foul swoop
your high pedestal comes crashing down,
never again will you feel the sun
breathe the air,
doomed to spend your time polished in a kitchen

or written on
and crumpled up.
Once mighty
now nothing.

Wake up
you're dreaming.
It's not too late
save yourself from yourself.

The Glory

Fearlessly the idiot faced the crowd, smiling
for he had seen the light over yonder,
never has someone traveled farther
for some goal that isn't tangible.

Push and pull as they must,
never will they hold the glory
but they're tale will be a magnificent story.

Facing the crowd he had a grin,
one that could match his need to win.
He need not open his mouth
the mountains released a great shout.

He floated up above them all,
from their eyes he was a hundred feet tall.
His hand flew at an incredible pace,
the wind swirled and he began to bend space.

Clouds began to form,
his talent was one not of the norm.
What was this trick
that is making the weather sick.

A white light blinded the crowd,
so amused and wowed.
They did not notice
like a great white lotus.

Snow began to fall from the air
the people ran around without care,
the ground was once bare,
but now it shimmers like the coat of a hare.

Fearlessly the idiot faced the crowd, smiling
for he had seen the light over yonder.
Never has someone traveled farther
for some goal that isn't tangible.

Push and pull as they must,
never will they hold the glory
but they're tale will be a magnificent story.
Templar Cheers

The quest for the grail
begins on this shadow trail.
Behind us stands the templar force,
two men riding one horse.
We must head to the holy land,
protecting travelers, slight of hand.

The church calls our bluff
but we have the good stuff.
Black mail of the holy,
what we've found could change the story.

The secrets of the game
are nothing but insane.
We hide behind our minds
and never think to unwind.
Work until we die
with nothing but money in our eyes.

The truth seeks ears
and here come the cheers,
because there are no more mirrors.

The Lights

Streetlights they watch like eyes,
darkness surrounds as the hills roll by.
Emptiness has the sweetest sounds
you just have to touch the ground.

Central vortex we are all one,
the lights circling
they shine on no one.
The voices whisper from beyond the darkness,
take the rainbow
out of this abyss.

I might be crazy
I might be insane,
this is just a passage into my brain.

Looking out the window watching the sun rise,
the gorgeous view only makes me the wise.
Waiting around like a couple of rocks
I'm just wasting away in the box.

I might be crazy
I might be insane,
this is just a passage into my brain.

I'm a golden owl
out on the prowl.
I never sleep
watch me leap.
From above it descended like magic fire,
moving the space around
running to the edge of the wire.
From where we stood it seemed to have no end,

but a voice boomed out
I'm your friend.

Lost in shock and awe
we were ready to grab our guns and draw,
but the voice was of a calming being.
It was greater than I was seeing.

I might be crazy
I might be insane,
this is just a passage into my brain.

Dream

The frozen wasteland,
death grip of nature's hand.
Still,
breezy.
Arctic fog across the landscape
for the sun I cannot wait.
Effortless flowers roll by
diamond of color in my eye.
Here comes the ancient tree
I wonder what he'll say to me.
The edge is drawing near,
it's just beyond the clear path lying ahead
watch where you tread.

Darkness fell
and we returned to our tents,
now we just have to imagine what that dream
meant.

Rolling down the bayou,
looking for a few
Cajun Queens
who know what I mean.
Jump in the boat my dear,
have yourself a beer.
We shall arrive soon,
lets stare at the moon.
Laying back
silence transports us,
no longer do we ride the bus.

Darkness fell
and we returned to our tents,

now we just have to imagine what that dream
meant.

There is nothing,
mindless desert.
Pigs wander through the sand,
all following one man's hand.
A promised land awaits,
fertile island
trees top mountains
ever closer to the fountain.
Don't sit back and let it take,
it will be a mistake.
One you'll think is fake,
one you never thought you'd make.
Mother stands back and laughs,
you just failed to do the math.

Darkness fell
and we returned to our tents,
now we just have to imagine what that dream
meant.
Will we ever know what the dream meant.

Test the waters my lady,
might we be clear to set sail.
My crew has waited two days.
We live to pillage and plunder,
but are kept inside
by this rain and thunder.

I'm getting sick
this weather treats me bad,
no better than you have.
Your body drives me mad,
it's sad. Just a tad,

so sad.
I stole you
from the bayou,
because it seemed fun
to live under the sun,
with a Cajun Queen
was that so mean?

You just want to be free.
It's in your eyes,
I despise
the look in your eyes.
Fake promises,
all lies.
All lies.

As darkness fell,
she cast a spell.
One to deliver her from this hell.

Settle In

A boat made of lost dreams,
riding on the edge of the seam.
Sunlight peaks over the horizon,
tapestry of red and yellow
cloak the land.
Touch the ground
feel it in the sand.
Ocean breeze
race through me,
let me become one with the sea.

Settle in
it's about to begin.
My dreaming Queen,
where are you?
Your words can't be true.
The sky tells you lies,
look up and be with fools
or look around
and listen to the ground.
Calling from inside
we continue to hide.
I'm waiting for the night watchmen,
He's got a secret plan and I'm a fan.

Bring about demise
I will save us from lies.
Crossing mountains
on a quest for the fountain.
It begins within.
Block out all those flashing lights,
bring in the darkness
to see the world's true might.

My Papa's Gone Whaling

My Papa's gone whaling,
across the mountain sky.
The river runs red,
as I sit here and cry.
The Queen is still missing,
villagers wonder why
their king continues to lie.
Sands of deserts
temples of holy,
stare into evermore.
We'll find the Queen someday
hidden in the floor.

A Mission of Falling

Drive the wagon,
I need to roll one
it's getting hot in the sun
and this rides only begun.

The trees whisper
in the distance I can hear,
the call of shadows
traveling horseman
wanders of Avalon
Ashley's Garden.
People cry out,
the doors caving in
you're ruining it with sin.

Memories and goodbyes
shrouded with lies.
Lost without the white warriors,
they're mission of falling
gave us the calling.

Time

How are you so white
bright,
it's impossible not to see your light.
The darkness contains every color,
what do you see?
Open the door
say hello to the shadow,
the aqueducts flow nocturnal
purple flames encase the city.
The tree yells
I want to kill you,
say the word
and it will be true.
Of all the colors we can see
we had to choose one,
TV.
Don't you see how it could be
we could live along side the tree.
Why have we gathered in this theater?
Did you want to sit back
and lose track.
Time
the great illusion.
Without it we are free
it's plain to see.
No rhyme, no time.
Bogged down in the slime,
I'm trapped by the grind
obeying time.

Pink Dreams

My Cajun Queen
visits me in my dreams,
she floats in the sky.

With fog surrounding
almost drowning.
Poisoned
by our glorious inventions.
We took order,
perfect creation,
and killed her.
Where is life
flowing through the hillside
now that the child takes over.
Given everything he could have ever wanted,
and poisoned it.
Dug us deeper into the pit.

There in the moonlight
she stands,
hair flowing
the moment seems right.

Look into the sky
as time passes you by.
Maybe you'll wonder why
they deceive us with lies.
She gives us a sign
as we sit here and whine.
Further down the line,
we'll wake up from our dream
and embrace the Cajun Queen.

Angel of the everglades,
show me just a shade of your magic beauty.

The life you live
runs along a different path,
flowing
hear a laugh.
There is something about the moon
floating like a balloon.
Worshiping the night
we have to wait for the light.
Stare into the darkness
bright.

A glow in the distance,
it's sad that you miss this.
Pink dreams
of Cajun Queens.

The Sun Doesn't Lie

Stay my butterfly
you float in the sky,
why do you cry.

Your home
is the greatest throne.
Stand tall
or you will fall, into
illusion
evolution.
Chaos
Babylon.

Build your tower,
I'll lay here and relax
oh look a flower.
When will you put down the axe?

Rise my Queen
experience the dream.
Look up into the sky
the sun doesn't lie.
Grow brighter in the glow,
I'll just listen to the wind blow.
It never seems to go fast,
dear lord
how time has past.

Mixing up the Medicine

Follow the wind's howl
listen for a vowel.
I and I is all there be
in the everlasting world of tree.
Without them we are done,
Mother Earth loses her fun.
No longer will blue and green
decorate the scene.
Do you know what I mean?

They're drawing near,
approaching the clear.
Midnight stallions
of the kings battalion
thunder towards me.
From the mountains
you can see,
the slaughter
of the tree.

Relax
put down the axe,
why tread the tracks
if you don't know the facts.

Ancient war parts the sea,
men at battle refuse to see,
what this world would be
if we no longer had the tree.

A Spanish mast
falls on the native past.
Never have we seen such bountiful lands,

but now it's in our hands.
I see no enemy that stands,
only peaceful native dwellers.
Lock them in the cellar.
Freedom will be our trick
so slaughter them all
before one stands up tall.

Rise my friend
this isn't the end.
Listen to them call out
from the valley
you hear a shout.
Overcast
brings rain at last.

Ancient war parts the sea,
men at battle refuse to see,
what this world would be
if we no longer had the tree.

See the face everywhere
into the clouds you stare.
The Cajun Queen's magic hair
flows like a watery flare.

The world looks desolate
we've made a mess of it.
There is only one way I see
us going back to how it used to be,
worship the tree.
Brothers you and me
must love the tree.
Run to the mountain
I hope you find the fountain.
Meet me in the garden of glory,

sit by the fire
and I will tell the story.

Ancient war parts the sea,
men at battle refuse to see,
what this world would be
if we no longer had the tree.

Ride the Snake

My thoughts are scattered across endless rainbow skies.
When I look down I see the pigs marching in line.
In the mirror they look and see angels.
To them this existence is all that matters.
They cannot see themselves,
they're minds are inflated.
Lost in an abyss.
They say deal with it,
this is the world we live in.
But I say no
this world can change.
We can all change.
We just have to see the true reason for change,
to get away from money and power.
They are evil.
The snake gives us life
but he gives us evil.
It is your choice.
We've been choosing evil for too long.
We must ride the snake once more
to find the truth.

Hear the Moon Call

The river flows under this starry night,
follow the moon's glow and turn black bright.
The woman stands
cringing over the counter.
Darkness is above
stars
listen to the fire
hear howls
distant mountain wolves
hungry
wanting
ride the river
call out to the mother.

Momma when's supper?
Four more days on the sea
and you no longer smile
we ride the mile.

Rugs on the wall
hear the moon call.

The child waited patiently
outside the dusty desert bar.
Mexican mountains
hilltop fountains.

Horses roam wild
capture the fire
women
I admire
your eyes of desire.

Run through the sand
flowing winds
father sun
the dance has just begun.

Climb Aboard the Train

Look into the forest
where wild creatures roam.
They tempt you away from your home.
Just play your guitar,
it will be your staff
lead with a laugh.
Honor awaits you at the pass,
make sure you don't run too fast.
At the end of the hall
lies my brain
endlessly going insane.
Climb aboard the train
I believe it's beginning to rain
or am I just going insane.

The Lonely Mountain

The elders laugh at the children as they play,
but they will rue the day
the young dethrone with a song,
those who stand in their way.

Charging down the stone path
hear them cry, hear them laugh,
the guards block the door, soon to be no more.
The child raises his oak staff

omitting a blinding light,
all the elders grew with fright.
Never will they see the day and watch the children play,
on a midsummers night.

Ride on to the next mountain
hear the water of the fountain,
arrows fly as men fall and die,
listen to the lonely mountain.

Light the eternal fire
up goes the funeral pier.
Dance around the flames
as we look for someone to blame.
On goes the shame
they think we're all the same.

Traveling on our journey
do you think you are worthy?

No matter the distance that spans between us,
we worship under the same sky,

don't let anyone tell you
you can't fly.

Anonymous

Lost we stood
the island was gone
that is why we sing this song.

There are men that die
on the hillside
and we sit here and hide
can't you hear them cry.

Fight for liberty
fight for our rights
fight until morning
until we see the light.

The Great American Lie
hear the troops battle cry,
in the sky the flag flies
but our pride never dies.

So long as a man sits on the throne
we will follow like drones,
breaking our bones
we stand like stones.

Drums are rolling
the bombs are now soaring,
I hear the voices
they are calling.

Follow me
I'm just going to run around here,
it's magical
fields of rainbows

awe
kaleidoscope.

Follow me,
you'd never guess what you'll see,
the tree
is waiting for you and me.

Tomorrow

White warriors fall
as you rise into the sky.
Shamanistic image
flashes by your eyes.
Stories
not yet told.
No one has been that bold.
But the divine voice
says you're making the right choice.
The others will linger in your heart,
they've been there from the start.
Honor and glory are yours,
just finish your chores.
One day of rest
in the Garden of Eden.
One day until
you can be seen again.
Rest
the maidens are out tending to the harvest.
Would you like a beer?
The ocean is just over this way.
Today is your lucky day.
For tomorrow
you will embark on a journey.
the morrow
brings sorrow.
For tomorrow
brings sorrow.

Arise
you are a mighty warrior.
Battle is about to be waged,
your body is filled with rage.

They've locked you in a cage.
When did we turn the page?
You must fight a bear,
they're everywhere.
Wonder why they stare,
just look at your hair.
Are we to be like Indians
and then,
never to be free again.
Use the earth to heal
not destroy,
but it gives them joy.
Those bloody bastards,
no one said they could be the masters.
This is the great disaster
it's what your life is after.
Save the children
we won't be free until when,
people live as one,
we are all the prodigal son.
Just wait
it's only begun

The Island

Peer around the corner,
gaze into the glare.
The light is shinning over there.
It's as if the wind is blowing
you can feel it in the air.
Travel to the island,
across the black sea.
Just leave me.
I will stay behind,
and relax my mind.
The darkness
is my only friend,
be with me until the very end.
Don't wait around,
I'm not going to send
back to town.
Your secret is safe with me,
no reason for it to flee.

Away in the distance,
I could see the shadows appear on
the
cold
dark
island.
Ghosts
they wandered the hillside,
edging closer to the light.
The blues had another plan,
swoop in at the last moment
it will be grand.
Scatter.
They are coming for you.

Lights flashing
bees flying by your head
thunder cracks in the distance.
The shadows begin to fall,
and as the last strike of lighting
exhausted the islands all mighty flame,
we all stood around looking for someone to blame.

The Being Returns

A shade of red
covered the town.
Where is the hero
everyone looks around.
Slain
in the dark night,
no one to guard by candlelight.
Call to the wizard
and all his might,
are you afraid of what lurks in the night?
Darkness falls, and
the being returns.
Blood will rain from the mass, wait
what is descending from the pass.

Lead Me

Amazed by all the racket
the man decided to take a stroll
through the town..
The path curved ahead
through forest
over streams
traversing valleys
but the man still walked it.
After a days walk
he thought maybe I'll leave the forest soon.
No said a bellowing voice from yonder.
You're going the wrong way.
Turn around.
Okay thank you.
The next day after more hours of walking
he came across a bridge.
Narrow
and paramount
he must cross.
Again a bellowing voice said
you are going the wrong way
there is another bridge down stream
this one has a loose beam.
Thank you again.
After weeks of walking
the man came to the edge of a valley.
Sheer cliff side.
This time a different voice came about and said
jump
do not be afraid
just do as I say.
Don't you know the third time is the charm?
But the man just sat down and closed his eyes.

I shall wait,
I am not ready.
Years passed
and the man didn't move.
Until one day as he was about to lose hope
the deep bellowing voice said
my friend,
why did it take you so long to realize
who I am
together to the end.

Dear Lord

Those little blue suits,
they have to choose blue.
Represent the vast sky above,
shun our
creative
mindless
earthly tour.
Lead us down the path covered in glass,
and tell us it's actually pillows.
The promised land waits on the other side of the
next dune,
until it has been surmounted
then the target moves on,
but each time we fall for it.
What a simple trick.
It makes me sick.
There is this Cajun Queen,
that is being mean.
Rejecting my advances
I'm not good enough.
Not smart enough.
Don't have a goal in life.
I just make a plant my wife.
But I have to tell you love,
it's sent from above.
We can ride the dove.
Fly away on our dove.
Lord I just want to move back to the Bayou,
I think my Queen misses it too.
Summer nights
below the lights
air runs strong
lets hit the bong.

Prepare the ship,
we shall leave for breakfast soon.
The sun will rise
yellow balloon.
Lord why do you give me such beautiful days
if there's no way to say
how you feel.
She's driving me insane,
there are too many voices in my brain.
It's like I'm riding the train
and everyone knows my name
but they look all the same.
Just give me the words
and I'll write them on the page,
maybe we can move them into a new age.

Your Dreamer

The Veil of Existence

Amazed
in front of the gates of slaughter
the people stood red with anger.
Eyes pierced the veil of existence
in their small village,
lost in a realm of time
they stood motionless
waiting to be called
one by one
they stepped into the mass
blood from the heavens.
Hear me call out my father
our existence ends soon
numbers rise
we fall.

Be a Friend

When the world seems its darkest
it's preparing for it's brightest.
Just hold on to life
there will be a light.

Plans greater than ever imagined,
your life is a pawn
no more than a game of chess,
all you wait for is dawn.

Tell me something my friends,
where is the road taking us?
It is endless, curving though the forest,
but in the end we must have trust.

The world knows all
and we know nothing,
it is our shadow leader
guiding us to one thing.

You'll never know your true purpose,
because in the end
it was staring you in the face,
live life and be a friend.

My Friend

The black snake sits in front of me
covered in white tribal tattoos
it ponders
it doesn't sense fear.
I invite it into my home
my reward is a bite on my forearm
but what do I care,
he is still my friend
but when people gather around
they say
that's poisonous
pointing to the snake.
What do you mean
I say as I look at my arm,
the bite had swollen into a purple golf ball.
Looking down at the snake
I shrugged
and said
oh well
it's over
I feel no pain,
and then I awoke.

Chariot Ride

Everyone wants me to be there
but I just want to be here,
locked in sweet serenity.
A new beginning, a new ending
an everlasting day
but never will I say
this is a promise,
it's a lie.
Look me in the eye
and you will see what I despise.
Here comes the chariot
gold wheels forever turning,
the horses are long gone.
For this is a ride of melancholy,
draw close to me now
the axel may break
and who knows
we might end up in the lake.
Too fast to judge
to slow to run,
can't you see
I'm just sitting here
having fun.

The Saber

Too much weight, from long days,
stand up tall, I'll show you the way.
Float effortlessly across the rainbow,
drift in the clouds,
show me the path in this world of laughs.
Find the saber walking along the cliff side,
around the old tree the road bends,
but where could this cat hide,
the saber is smart, it must be where the track isn't
the trend.

Lost in a Sea of Frustration

I.
Locked in a future moving path
no time for a laugh.
Run endlessly in the place I roam
I have no time to stay home.

The pressure is on to win
no way to the top without sin.
Listen to your leader they say it's your turn,
but sadly you're the butt of the burn.

The games are beginning
the ceremony is riding the wind.
The bells ring through the valley
the storm is howling sally.

II
Gliding along smooth caverns
you spot a ghoul and a beast
residing for a feast.

Drawing upon one's sword
for an ounce of courage
to fight the spiritual battle.

They take a drink from the well of wisdom
trading an eye for a morsel of wealth.
Don't you know it's good for your health?

III
The air is crushed under elephants,
men die waiting for their turn.

Lost in a sea of frustration,
we sit on padded blue and burn.

False pleasures to speed up time,
I think I am losing my mind.
No way to unwind
when the man puts down our kind.

Old and new we sit
walking through the lines,
falling deeper into the pit
at the bottom waits our fine.

She is Crying

We are this world's greatest creation
bound to destroy our mother.
Warpath
annihilation
we speed on towards our destination
never looking down or around
why see the day when you can see tomorrow
it's as if time was irrelevant
only the future
how can what will happen matter more than now?
Nature and the human existence
we chase our mother around the fire
laughing
she is crying
dancing
we are rejoicing
success
we have killed her
silently
she kills us.

An Undiscovered Goddess

Search
search
search all you want
you'll never find the answer,
because I found you first
blindfolded you
and told you to find me
even though I follow
your every footstep
waiting for you to become aware
of what's truly going on.
An undiscovered goddess
stands there commanding her lion herd.
At the ready
roaring
waiting
dinner is coming soon
we just have to wait for the moon.

The Marching Band

Close your eyes
stop reading this poem
and imagine nothing.
Block out all sound
only feel the blood
coursing through your body.
How does it feel?
You are becoming a human again.
Those things you waste your days with
mean nothing when your blood stops flowing.

On the far shore
only experience matters.
You cannot bring anything across the river
but what you have locked in your mind.
The ferryman relieves you of all possessions
and leaves you with a clear mind.
Not even your body is aloud across the way.
So live today.

The marching band
moves at the wave of my hand
trampling all
that encroach my land.
Six beams of light
ride the skyline
into a golden field
of Alaskan pine.
The hammer drops
ten leagues below
the monkey's brow,
and the judge is astonished
but how?

Silver spoon lining
our coal table,
does self-destruction
really need a label?
My internal lube is legal
but my mental release is illegal.
It's a steep slope
denying people dope.

A Quest for Endless Glory

Along the savannah travels a medicine man,
A hive of bald face floats above his hand,
Entering a village that had just been pillaged,
He says to the people, would you like some inspiration,
From the hive he draws a herb and gives it to all the people,
Take this and rejoice, the earth has given you a voice,
It's the beginning and the end, it's our only friend,
Banished by the confused, accepted by the wise,
The truth is clouded by lies,
Take this herb and follow me,
And I will show you what this world is meant to be,
This life we live is one big story,
A quest for endless glory

A Veil of Innocence

Slyly he makes his way from the bushes,
nodding goodbye to his back yard prostitute.
She lays open in the field
with a veil of innocence covering her groin,
waiting for her next midnight rider.

In the Pig Pen

I play to feel the energy
the worlds grace flows through my fingers.
Sound becomes colors
inverting perception,
of our self-conscious minds.

Save us from eternal damnation,
may hellfire and brimstone be swept aside
unless we cannot see the light.
Our mother waits for us on the wharf,
hell's boat eagerly bides until we are ready.

Killing daily
the king's men.
Lock away
in the pig pen
all of your evil emotion.

In an Endless Game

Trapped behind a bamboo curtain
I am watching the world retrogress.
The people are laughing
oblivious to there secret disruption.
Hail to the mother
the father
those that birthed us from
the ashes of creation.
We set the fields of our birth on fire
with our "beautiful" creation.
Each one makes living easier
but eliminates part of the experience.
Our minds progressively shut off
as less is required of them.
Hail to the king
ruler of our land
guiding us with just a simple swing of a hand.

The willow a-flame
no one to blame
it's all the same
in an endless game.

Remove Oppression

Take away every thing you've ever known,
remove oppression
human creation
language
race
nations.
Anything that separates
is destructive.
We will never be able to completely remove evil,
but hopefully one day there will be more moral
people
then unjust.

Bears Dance with the Elves

We gather in this grim hall of sorrows,
declaring that the dead will live on tomorrow.
No more suffering
no more pain,
we've lost a man
and have all to gain.
His knowledge passed onward
through the golden gates he walks forward
greeted by past lovers,
living in a place without sorrow.
We will meet again tomorrow.

Awake
ruins along a foggy stream.
Breeze running through the swamp grass.
Hear forest dwellers playing drums,
a centennial procession is going on over yonder.
What could they be celebrating?
Walk edge closer.
See the torches lit
a grand bonfire
ten feet tall.
Bears dance with the elves
to a barbarian beat.
Silence
the drums stop.
Footsteps on rose pedals,
a man proceeds into the center of the celebration.
Welcome they all shout.
We have been waiting for you,
this is all for you.
You have left the lower realm to dance forever in
the moonlight.

Resident king
it's your turn to sing.
He responds
thank you.
My family is sad
but if they could see what awaits on the other side
maybe they would smile.
Give it a while
as some pass more are born.
The cycle continues
the life force moves on.

Your Magic Aura of Alcoholic Funk

Your password is incorrect
you're not allowed in here.
Why are you trying to get in
we have all the time in the world.
Your magic aura of alcoholic funk
draws me closer into your arms.
Baby there is no reason for alarm
in our moon light shelter from the storm.

Crawl

The path stretches past the old oak,
rambling
there is a wall.
Jump
climb
crawl
beg
love.
The other side brings glory
you know the rest of the story.

We Have Won

Hey people
grab your swords
were going to cut down our mother
in search of a non-existent crown.
Nothing shall be natural all will be forgot.
Ramble along the paved path
over the grave of nature.
How can we live through each slow day
watching her bleed out
like a deer on the side of the road.
We stand aside and cry
without ever thinking to do something.
Just because we don't live as long as our world
doesn't mean we can slaughter it and leave a carcass
for the future residents.
Would you like to be raped and left to die for a
million years?
It took the victim four billion years to stand tall
and only two thousand for the murders to kill it.
Thank you my friends for your assistance in the
hunt.
We have won
if you can call this winning.

Reality Has Become Digital

I'm disgusted by this generation
this world we live in,
where your digital appearance is all that matters.
Personal interaction is lost,
our minds follow a unmarked larger plan.
We walk along a path of no return
where you share everything via the internet.
Patience is gone
reality has become digital.
We no longer appreciate out earth,
only what we've created on top of it.
Doesn't anyone see the world around us?
Have you not experienced its beauty?
I am lost in what to do,
our new world draws me in
as the old world calls to me for help.
If you understand my message
join me in this fight for life.
We are killing our existence daily
with our beautiful creations.
How can you think we are meant to destroy
when we have the ability to create.
We are our god
we are the father
we are the mother
we are the son.
Can you see we are inches from a final conclusion?
Our beauty is meant to unite the world,
we are the peacekeepers.
I'm sick of people saying this is how it is,
what are you going to do about it?
One person can change a nation.
Rule the world.

Don't you see they have realized this and thrown a
sheet over our eyes?
They are afraid of us
because we are strong if united, but
so long as we stay divided
there is no hope for our existence,
on this earth we have been blessed with.

Does it Make Sense?

Have we succeeded in removing nature as the apex
predator?
She can no longer concur our god
technology
medicine
it's all fake
we're drowning in the lake.
Once an ally
this world is our enemy
constantly trying to win us over
while we say no.
We shall cut you down
humans rule all
thumbs
make us bums.
Tools
drool.
Does it make sense
to go against what created us?
You constantly kill your God
and then ask why he betrays you.
Pollution
is not the solution.
There are no gods
there is nothing,
only a ominous living world
calling for us to be one,
how it used to be.
Go back to our birth
afraid of all,
not protected by our
chaotic creations.
Relying on our mother and father

infantile
find your roots
you are a tree,
explore the sea
you are a dolphin,
roam the savannah
you are an elephant,
touch the ground
you are the earth,
so find some worth
return to your birth
and love the earth.

II
Your Cute Little Nose Inspires Poetry and Prose

I Stand Alone

Your love
fits like a glove,
but my love
why do you fly away
riding a dove.

As a poet I stand alone
people see me on a throne,
but I sit on a stone,
cold and alone.

Where is my fair queen?
She stands between
me and my dream.

If only I could say three words to thee,
I would be so much better off mentally.
It's plain to see
you don't want me.
You know this doesn't seem,
like that first night
we laid together and dreamed.
Down pour
no more.
The river runs red in the moonlight,
don't be afraid
shadows lurk out of sight.
I might look like a bore,
but just wait and see what I have in store
for our midnight
river ride
on the east side.

As a poet I stand alone
people see me on a throne,
but I sit on a stone,
cold and alone.

Where is my fair queen?
She stands between
me and my dream.

My queen of the black sea
stands on the beach
and waits for me.
Her ship sails across the sky
the birds chirp and cry,
do you wonder why
the day passes by.
Silk skin
where have you been.
Your cold caress
causes distress.
My body aches for your touch,
just a bit too much.
Soft eyes
no lies
don't cry
it's only goodbye.

Soft kiss
grim lips
oh how I miss
my baby's lips.

The Wrong Side of the River

This girl
one I want to twirl,
floating across the dance floor
I begin to implore,
my love for her hand
we could rule the land.
King of Dreams
and the Cajun Queen.
Side by side
rulers never divide.

Born on the wrong side of the river
the almighty sliver.
Harsh times
bring terrible people,
set the mine
awake beneath a new steeple.

You shine like a pearl,
possibly the perfect girl.
An elegant Cajun Queen,
one of my many dreams.
Look at me
for I see a shade
of a color never before made.
Your eyes
are all the wise,
they've been told countless lies.

Elizabeth

Faster
we tear into the nightmare,
unbuckle your luck
waste a buck
in the jukebox of sorrow
wait until tomorrow.
Why love today
when tomorrow you will play.
My love is at the end of the line
smiling she sees me
I look away
afraid of something so beautiful.
She doesn't understand
my plan.
Artistically
I wait and see
what will come to me.
words they flow like the sea
poems bide before they can be.

Dionysus unite us
free us
from this world of the damned.
God of the vine
help us to unwind,
lead the train
drive the bus
enter our brain
in wine we trust.

The lines are blue
strung pride and true
at the top of the tower

she calls down to me
when can we be
together and free.
My love it's plain to see
I just need to climb this tree.
My weeping willow
caressing pillow
cries out to you
your eyes of blue.
Don't cry
I would never lie
to a beautiful face
look behind
I leave a trace
of sunset colors
riding the breeze
my train flies with ease.
Dancing through fields
waving wands and shields
no battle to be waged
only omnipresent anti-rage
and at the end of the page
cry out to the sage.

The Embers

The embers
I can still remember
they illuminated your
soft warm face
as I laid a hand on your cheek
your body let out a shriek.

Fire and ice we were that night
we gave the world a fright
your eyes shinned so bright
under the moonlight.

The car cruised
pacing the birds
beachside
ocean breeze
waves crashing at our feet
you jumped into my arms
frozen
our hearts were warm
we took shelter from the storm.
You let out a slow breath on my neck
I kissed your forehead
and laid you to bed.

Do you remember that night?
Sand between our toes
kisses on the nose
reciting prose,
you were in my arms
there was no reason for alarm
in between our dreams
we broke the seam.

No Direction

Reflections
affections
no direction
to my queen.

Fantasies
as I stare into your eyes.
I will wait in line all day
just for a chance to say
hello.

Mysteries
lurk between us,
who will make the move?
A lion I am afraid
lets take shelter
from the air raid.

Only the Brute

Love
is a dove
that flies wingless
through swamps,
falls like feathers
crushing people
softly into pancakes.

She says no.
Your heart and soul
tossed
salad
tomatoes
juiced
ketchup
on your Sunday.

You walk away.

Broken
the war has just begun
this is where it starts to be fun.

She caresses your cheek
with her eyes
lies
she lies.
It is not you she wants
only the
brute
brainless and dead.
The one who
builds a wall

of governmental prose,
following rules
declaring hatred of the rules.
Never will he ever stand
only follow the crowd's hand.

Love Notes: Volume One

I.
Close your eyes child
the world around us is wild,
but the fire is warm
it will protect us from the storm.

II.
Be a child, run free.
Feel the warm summer air through your soft
flowing hair.
These days
I run bare and
don't even care.

III.
I want to
hold you tight by the moonlight.
Caress your soft skin
as the waves crash on the shore,
whisper in your ear
do you want more?

IV.
Your eyes are the prize I wish to obtain.
I hear the train rolling in
as the day ends
a new one begins,
without you
it would be a sin.

V.
She is a roman statue,
carved from the finest marble.

Magical mountains
coat her landscape.
In my rearview
I can see the legendary behind,
her past is as long as a ship's mast.

VI.
You are queen of the moon
who rises high above all,
shining bright
her mystical hair
flows without a care.
Eyes that pierce iron armor,
a stare that make men cry,
a body carved out of stone,
she's hardly ever alone.

VII.
A cool breeze crawls upon my neck
and I'm sorry to wreck
this little game you play.
It's too bad I can't stay
but I can't live this way.
When they're calling me to do more
my feet are planted to the floor,
and I have plenty in store
for this little game you play.

VIII
You're an angel from Avalon
who dances with fire in the midnight sky.
A princess that spins the world around on her finger,
caressing glances from yonder bringing glee.
She stands before all and they see
what beauty is meant to be.

With a Carless Glare

Her soft face speaks softly under the night sky,
follow me into the ever loving abyss.
Beauty can try and tame the beast, but
only in the night shall he succumb to her awe-
inspiring beauty.

With a careless glare
she melts his battle-hardened heart.
Tearing away at the wounds of the women who
came before.

Golden Runes

The stars a-lined
to link our births
under the midnight moon.
The gods traversed countless valleys
to find all of the golden runes,
only on the night they were all joined together
would the moon shine brighter than the sun,
beginning the universe's greatest unity.

I Fly Nocturnal

Rain falls on the window
dreams flow down the street
hoping to one day meet
a lionhearted lover.

Dirt road
along the shear cliff,
don't look down
you may drowned.

Gloomy trees
bright shadows,
shaking knees
yellow grass.

Mountains in the distance
the moon flies low,
black as day
do you hear what I say.

I need a release
I'm begging
my queen
to leave
my dreams,
and join me
in this puzzling world.
She thinks I'm set
but I'd bet
I know nothing.

As an owl
I fly nocturnal,

search for my prey
night and day.
She hides
in a tree,
find the axe
cut her open.
Count her rings.
She lies
it doesn't fly
tell me the truth,
do you want me?
I want you.

Distance is nothing
only a number,
time is an illusion.
Days are minutes
as years are seconds.
So when I find you
all will end,
inspiration you are
but why are you so far.

It Started at Birth

Sailing across a diamond sky
she wonders why,
all of the people refuse to see
the true meaning of we.
Together we are this earth
it started at birth
alone we have no worth.
Stand and fight
until the morning light
when the moon grows dark
and the sun bright.

Ivy Eyes

Ivy eyes
are her disguise,
caressing every man she see's
with her ivy eyes.

Emerald worm holes
that envelop all light
drawing attention
do I dare mention
her behind,
it helps me unwind.

She waits on the shore
saying
there has to be more.
His passion is drawn out
when he writes and
tries to scream and shout.

Baby your ivy eyes
are all too wise
for my midnight disguise.

Your Golden Locks

Your soft glare
runs without care,
silk skin
caressing
depressing
how distance can ruin perfection.
Your golden locks
are the building blocks
behind my eternal creation.
Oh beautiful maiden
in my dream you laid in my bed beside me
and we rode the sea.
Turn around
feel it in the ground,
this earthquake
doesn't it make you
want to dance forever
and always be together.

Aimless Verse From 83'

She stands there
with her flowing hair
and chest so bare.

Guarding a secret
it's so hard for her to keep it,
but all I want to do
is be with you.

Your bodacious mountains
I want to traverse.
Reach the mystery piercing
do you like my verse.

Says the Dark Queen

Says the dark queen
as she steps out into the radiant moonlight.
He fingers caress an arrow
covered in blood.
Drawing it back
she is reminded of the pain from lost souls of yester year.
They were crushed under her majestic feet
in a battle so fierce
ravens flew on winds away from the grounds.

Lioness of My Dreams

Purple shadows
stretching over my head
this is the day I dread.
There is no more
maiden who I adore.
Your lips taste divine
how are you so fine,
lay by me and we can unwind
you can listen to my moon driven mind.

Oh how she crawls from the darkness,
low lying back
golden fur
she's hard to track
in this golden world.

The stars ignite this night
your eyes shine so bright
under this glowing moon light.

Babe don't be afraid
I will guard you from the raid,
all I want are your lips
soft
sweet
night time kiss.

Queen of the animals
lioness of my dreams
baby can you see
this world isn't what it seems.
Come live with me
in this old oak tree.

Your Voice isn't Choice

She used to laugh at me,
why do you always try and serenade me?
How will you sing?
Your voice isn't choice
and your words don't need to be herd.
Oh my love why do you betray me while at sea,
you know I was idly waiting for thee.
You wanted to be the writer
I was just a lover,
but now I am above her.
Laugh all you want
your love doesn't haunt
my dreams anymore.

The King's Flowers

Your blue eyes caress the setting sun
my longing for you has only begun.
Oh the way mountains dress the black sea
the moonlight is waiting for you and me.

Why do your run from the sun
we stand on top of towers
gardens
the kings flowers.

The Horizon of Lost Souls

Her castle looms over the horizon of lost souls,
wizards and warriors battle for her fair hand,
the river runs like lava, the bridge is guarded by a troll
and you know she's already decided who will rule the land.

All along the gorge, eagles sores so high.
Their feathers guide the journey through the sky.

Sierra

Her doom and gloom
run around the room
but I tell you this
the sun will break through soon.

It takes a while
for your smile
to appear
on my file.

You tread through the marshes
by the water side
staring at the sky above
wondering why the sun hides.

I can't wait around
and watch this world crumble
into the depths of hell
can you hear the thunder rumble.

She leads a angelic army
covered in rose thorns
they charge into battle
at the sound of the horns.

A ship follows behind
riding an ocean breeze
flags flying high above
they concur all with ease.

Her medallion
is her saving grace
ancient river soul
will help her win the race.

Girl don't cry
you know why
they lie
and make things up on the fly.

Our Endless Night Crawl

I didn't expect you
to be so beautiful.

But why do you hide
as I sit here and bide.
The gods shaped your face
your eyes make my heart race.

Stars cloak your cheeks
they make my legs weak,
for brief seconds that we talked
you tore through my heart like a hawk.

Baby you make rainbows wish they were waterfalls,
I wish we could dance forever in this hall
this could be the never ending night crawl.

I walk this lonely stone path
in search of a Cajun queen,
love do you ramble in the bayou
through the misty swamps of my dreams.

Let me know when you reach the castle
I will be waiting inside for you,
we can stay here forever without any hassle
so long as the river runs true
we can sing the blues.

Our endless night crawl
where the water falls
in Valhalla's mighty hall
you will be my queen.

My Queen Bee

She's floating there my queen bee
on display for all those to see,
crying out to her servants
to bring her more wine
but they say she's had enough
she's more than fine.
Babe you don't need anymore wine.

Trying to block out all of her troubles
throw away the key and be locked in a bubble,
buzz freely around the flowers
never again trapped in that tower.
Lets fly away my baby
ride the sky with our wings
our little wings of rainbow
the forest wants us to sing.

Your the queen
I'm the king
so sing to me babe,
let that little heart flutter
your voice is as smooth as butter.
Trees bloom to end the worlds doom
as you zoom
across the radar.

The cops can't stop you
your just a buzzing bee
beautiful and free
that's all you ever wanted to be,
classless and free.

I Decree to Thee

To all the women of the world,
I believe I am mentally insane
so feel free to join me
in this cozy world I call my brain.

The skies of blue
run red and true,
I think me and you
meld like glue.

It's all just bliss and forgiveness
in the land of love,
oh look a dove.
Stare into my mind of darkness.

It's All a Dream

Think about rainbows
waterfalls,
laying on a beach by a lover.
Warm sand
smooth ocean breeze.
He grabs your hand,
looking into you eyes
he says,
love
take me away from this wasteland.
Let us be free over the horizon.
I can't live through each slow day
just to feel that the years have flown by.
And you say,
be calm babe
we have until sundown to rejoice in this paradise.
When the moon takes the throne
we shall return to the festival.
Island drums beats
and blood curdling screams.
It's all a dream.

III
Hear the Call Above it All

Out of Bounds

Friends
from the end.
Calling
endless waving.
Say hello,
how's it been.
I remember when
I was where you stand
reaching out for a hand,
you look so grand.
We had to be perfect,
self reliance wasn't worth it.
Sent on a quest
spanning thousands of years,
if only we knew
the crown would be of tears.
They say it's an art form
but our life is nothing of the norm.

The ground you stand on is round,
your mind makes too many things
                              out of bounds.

The sky isn't blue
it's black.
I'm telling you
don't look back.
The colors are saturated
as the god takes his throne,
look around
do you really feel alone?
Inside you
is everything you've ever known.

Vast as the stars
we lock it behind bars.
It's given us a clue
stare into the ominous blue.
For when the night casts on a green horizon,
all will be as it should
endless.

An Old Oak Tree

An owl
I know nothing
Voices in the night
haunting.
Blues
are in the air
bring me down,
see if I care.
Her eyes
shown red with blood.
The dreamer couldn't believe her,
she wanted to kill me.
I ran into the mountains
in search of the fountain,
but as you can see
all I found was my mind
and an old oak tree.

The Observer

I find that when I am my most reserved
the people around me become open and inviting.
The strong does nothing
because he knows
the weak will break.
The common man knows not silence,
they need communication.
So when one decides to exclude themselves,
be different,
they are something that is questioning.
People are enamored by strange.
The man that sits
and observes
draws the most attention.
Everyone waits for
the few
precise
and calculated
words
eager to be released.

Mankind's Only Secret

If a picture is a thousand words
then my eyes are an eternity of speech.
Trying to capture in a photo
what I can see through my eyes
is impossible.
It's not only the image
but the thoughts that coincide.
How can one describe fog with a picture?
In my eyes
I see distortion
and mystery.
A photo
only reveals a blurry landscape.
Thoughts are the driving force behind life.
It's mankind's only secret.
No one can know your thoughts
unless you verbalize
or write them down.
The amount of excess thought wasted
is unfathomable,
the cure for cancer
was probably invented
in ones mind as a joke
and never published.

People are afraid of their minds.
They are drawn to the strange things in life
unless they come from themselves.
Dare to be different
because the common man's greatest fear
is to not belong.
To be an outcast is death
but to me

being an outsider is new life.
You are alone
and no one's opinion matters.
Be strange
that's how we got to where we are.
The first person to say
hey lets do this
was ridiculed
until he showed everyone
the error of their ways.

Reflections of Our Meager Existence

Reflections of our meager existence
blips on a galactic radar.
Maps of our lives
are lines on the side of skyscrapers.
So where does this feeling
of being owed something come from?
We just sit around
and wait
it will come,
we deserve it because
I am me
better than you
yet they think they are better than you.
As humans
have we forgotten we are just animals?
No different than you
lazy house pets,
our only advantage is our thumbs.
Most if not all animals can talk to each other
but we are left to talk to other humans,
our "massive" brains
what a shame
they ruin us
thinking more
killing from within.
Meager food for souls forgotten
said the wise man
locked in an existence
that we can't understand.

Sex Over All

Celebration has turned into a pig slaughter
sex over all
money
power.
Why do the most obscene thing
call us
advantages over another?
Disadvantages to ourselves
anything you do for
sex, money or power
will kill you.
When Lucifer gave us the light
he gave us the dark side
beauty can only be so
when compared to ugly,
so goes it for all.
It's sad but evil will always exist
but the hope is that there will be
more good people than bad.
I remember long ago when
I could walk outside and
say hello to a stranger and they
would say good day.
Now a-days people walk around
with their noses so high in the air
they don't even look at you.
Polite is stricken from the dictionary,
we are thrown in the gas chamber for
obeying a code of honor.

A World Without My Pen

I throw my money away
throw it right into the bay.
Watch it float out to sea
let the sharks run free.

How can I stop their slaughter
my beautiful girl
they've bought her.

Dragging her out to the field
she's crying
               let me be
I created you and me.

How can you stop the rhinos?
They charge on though the wall
gather the people
               and stand tall.

We may lose a few men
but I don't want to live
in a world without my pen.

The American High

Laying in a forgotten field
gazing
into the vast unknown.
Dogs sore like comets
aura of ghosts
glow like stars.
Milky way highway
horses in the theater
afraid of the snow storm.
War film
hooves sliding across thin ice
tanks crawl like legless dogs.
The radio kicks in,
this is my land
this is your land
from California
to the New York highway
cut to
soviet propaganda
American lies
feel the American high.
Don't you remember
this all happened before.
Awake.

We are Cult Followers

There is death behind the door
here it creaking through the floor.
The handle is shaking
your hand is quaking,
in fear
shed a tear
run my child
back into the wild
hide like you do now.
The world is crumbling
and you don't even raise a brow,
how?
Pagan rituals
we are cult followers
back to the Earth
to the place of our birth.

Half Thoughts

I
We live in this land of 4 by 4 trucks
and muscle cars.
We have to flaunt our creations
even if it destroys our world.

II
The final ounce of courage descended upon me,
as the light of guidance was extinguished.

III
Live for today,
learn from yesterday
and be thankful for tomorrow.

IV
Did you know we are ruled by our phones?
Walking around mindless like drones.
I tell you it is chilling my bones,
the computer has taken the throne.

We Owe it All to the Sun

Everyone lives in tomorrow
even though they say,
that you only live once
live it like it's your last.

So when you ask them about their future
a plan
for the next 4 to 10 years,
most give aspirations of schooling,
but if you are one who says
I'm not sure what I'll be doing tomorrow
than you receive
disappointed looks.

Why haven't you thought about your future?
Planned daily movements,
designed a way to make money.

Because that doesn't matter to me.
I want the experience,
the thrill of each day.
Life loses it's fun
when you forget
that we owe it all to the sun.

Fingertip Picking

Cottonwood
tall it stood,
only love could
concur all.
Jump off
free fall
hear the call
pass me the ball.

The son bends over
houses
tree tops
dormant people
dogs.
They are afraid to embrace
their magnificent world.

She says no.
Fingertip picking
trying not to get dirty,
ew
nature
I am above
your dirt filled existence.
I am not animal,
not instinctual.
Well then you refuse
the corner stone.

No Mercy

Are we so power hungry
that we need to concur nature?
Belittle what can not respond.
Since we have completely won
we move on to people,
but what we never thought
is happening.
She has found her voice.
Now is the time of her revenge.
Conjuring all of her power
she will give us
what we have given her,
no mercy.

The Prison is Calling Me

The air is still
on this eerie summer night.
Shadows are frozen
in the cool midnight breeze.
This prison is calling me
to leave the grounds
in search of a new forgotten land,
in which peace is the only ruler.
No gods or beliefs
only sprits living as one
under a compassionate sun.

Watchmen

Tall
strong
ancient
all knowing
father figure
watchmen
shadow warrior
peace keeper
life giver
yet somehow
our enemy.

A Life That Contains More

Is it weird for me
to have a feeling that
I am destined to live
a life that contains more
than the average school,
work, family, death.
I see corruption
I see pain
I see promise,
am I insane?
A voice calls to me from
the far shore,
save us.

The Answer is on the Ground

Oh mama where are we going?
Why can't the light
shine over here?
It's so far
yet so near.
I'm waiting for a clear in the clouds
so the moon can shine out loud,
proclaim glory
so I can write his story.
We are the only creature
who sits and stares at the stars
when the answer is on the ground.

The Demon

As this demon rips through my stomach
I am lost in a labyrinth of exile.
Without love
without pain
without life,
an abyss where only my thoughts live.
I have been locked in this prison
since the demon entered my realm.
I am happy that it joins me at the table
for it brings meaning
in my meager existence
on this dark majestic Earth.

Technicolor Boxes

The embers
I can still remember
how life once was.
Respect to another man
even if you had never met.

People have always been crazy
but your false worlds
trapped in Technicolor boxes
pushed them of cliffs.

Elephant pull from
handheld devices.

To our children
the physical world
means nothing,
only the cloud
that contains Johnny's photos
from the beach
and what Katie is up to.

We were all good people once.

The Trees of Our Forefathers

Be free sweet child of the stars,
ramble endlessly through the trees of our
forefathers
in search of something that has already found you.

Your quest is one we must all go through,
to find what the world has wanted all along
in our short joyous lives.

Victims of the Circumstance

If you control sex you can rule the world.
When you choose who reproduces
your favorite will always win.
Natural selection
tainted from what we want
not what the world needs.
We are victims of the circumstance
blatantly ignoring the answer
that stands at the other end of the hall,
one hand extended from the beginning of time.
Our problem solving had a purpose
until we chose otherwise,
but the man at the other end of the hall left us a doorway.
One in which we can enter to see the past,
one where we had no selection.

Bar Strategy

And they stood on the horizon waiting,
the sea crashed along the shore.
You may think I'm a bore
hopeless and more
I walk through the door
just to sit and ignore
your advances.
This tactic makes you want me
its plain to see
the way to catch a women you don't know
is not care.

Someone to Blame

Gradient of black to black,
it is a
vast
radiant
darkness.
Dots of distant life,
gorgeous gases of yester year show today.
We stand on this earth in competition, why?
Lets kill each other for personal gain!
No matter how you look at it
its all the same.
We just look for someone to blame.

Are We the Teenager?

You know we are the creation of this world,
so than why do we constantly rebel in a destructive matter?
Are we the teenager who hates his parents?
Forever destined to "know everything"
yet constantly learn.
Our mother is calling us
she wants us to come back into the forest.
We can dance forever on the mountain side,
please stop hiding and biding.

A Little Game They Call Life

Television is a vacuum that sucks your soul out
through your eyes.
Gorilla gripping your attention,
turning away is futile.
Listen to what I tell you.
The invisible forces
from a top the hill
control your mind
with a little game they call life.
Competition.
Beat your neighbor and you will be prosperous.
As humans we believe that we are above nature,
but in reality we are controlled by it.
No matter how many times we say
humans are above all
we must realize we are on the bottom of the ladder.
Destined to spend eternity
searching for something that's already found us,
for we refuse to see our grand mother caressing our
every movement
in this vast dream.

Drunken Chronicles

Lubed up with their hops
they converse about days when life was grand
and they were rulers of the land.

I can feel the back of my eyes
numb from hops and liquor.
Oil for my joints
moving is so easily
around the party.

Stab your past lives with sorrow
about why we don't live tomorrow,
and borrow a key
to unlock the door
into evermore
where all is endless.

An Over Beaten Cow

I really don't want any of this anymore,
tautened
meat
hung from the rafters
we walk through the butcher's shop
in search of our cut
only to find a over beaten cow
that was raped and slaughtered.
Do we not understand?
Are we truly so lost?
There are so many great people
but all of the terrible ones have the power.
When did we lose our leaders of valor
our knights of armor
samurai of honor.
When did we lose our morals?

For Too Long She Has Sat Dormant

Are you alive?
Lets get away from this
cold
dark
world
that betrays us.
We are beautiful
but those people
who have weaseled their way into power
are not.
They plot against us.
Conspire false operations to betray us.
Destroy what meager existence we have left,
but do you know who has our side?
The mother.
She created us
and she can destroy us.
For too long has she sat dormant
waiting for us to realize
that we can live in harmony.
There shall never be peace on earth until mankind
can be at peace with its creator.

Mother help us
Father forgive us
Brother and sister stand with us
in this final battle for love.

Blue Flame

There is a side
that tries to hide.
You can never see me
when I'm in my tree,
writing
prophesizing
imagining
contemplating.
I just look up at our impossible ceiling
never present
changing colors
blue flame
tame
the same
lights
my purple sky
I wonder why
eyes closed
shivering before I fall.

IV
Ascending into Asgard

The Call

Where is this journey taking me?
Somewhere I can finally be free.
I think I am edging close to see,
what I am truly meant to be.

A knight on the outside,
a poet trying to hide.
A samurai of the mind,
a judge just trying to unwind.

Will I continue on and answer the call,
or will I get caught up in the lime light and fall.
The choice is mine and mine alone,
I'm the one who has to answer the phone.

Runic Translations

I
The crown is upon your head my son,
run without a gun.
See the blue
above it all.
Stay pride and true
you can jump the wall.
You can't fall
when your above the ball.

II
Lord guide us on this endless quest
to fill the air with vibrating color.

III
Diamond
a gracious beach
lines these times
when all is gone,
we have lived a slow century.
Captured the treasure
at the end of a hero's quest.
Raised hell
and never asked for rest.

IV
May love shine bright
on the darkness of our morals.

V
Winds of my forefathers
drive me onward,
may I have the courage of a lion
and the compassion of a saint.
Let this life bring joy to all
before the day I fall.

VI
The voices call me from the stars,
play with us in eternal bliss
you don't know what you miss.
An orange light fades to green
at the end of this daily scene
and becomes blue
only when the sky is true

Princess of the Daunting Waters

The way to make
a castle crumble, is to
pray to the gods
hear the thunder rumble.
Crossing bridges into the dark realm,
the thick sea fog is rising above the helm.
Hoist up the sails
listen to the wails.

Princess of the daunting waters
do you ever falter.
Island
black sand,
dormant father
who's blood flows
when the gods tremble.

Galloping to the Gallows

Zebra on the outback
galloping to the gallows,
his brother waits
dour faces watch.

Ocean waves of emerald grass
parts to a sun filled scene.
Gloomy faces await
this man's fate,
I hope his brother isn't late.

Hail to the Stars,
Those Who Set the Bar

I
Praise to the mighty priestess
she calls for battle.
Pigs run on the street
when the answer is right at our feet.
Pillage our own villages
in a quest to annihilate the rest.
Runes gather dust
in the obscure trunk
I smell a skunk.

II
I worship you
oh powerful sun.
Warning the world
in your beautiful ways.
Caress the air we breath
move our eyes
across the sky
watching the time go by.

III
The moon takes her throne
covered in jewels,
she watches the cool night
along an isle of fools.
Dance in the hunt.

IV
Oh worshiper of the moon
why do you stand alone?
I follow my leader to the t
so maybe one day I can be
like the man who sits in the tree.
Above all
he rides the night
caste into the position of a life time
forever destined to know only darkness.

V
Your tiny minds don't understand
the secret lie of the leader.
Hail to the king of wine
mantra of the ecclesiastic.

A Man in Moss

I was rambling through the bayou,
when I came across a man covered in moss
and he said,
"Do you want to know the secret of the universe?
Take this path past the castle and around the heavens of Avalon.
There you shall find a stepping-stone with three jewels.
Waiting there and it will come."
What will?
But when I turned back he was gone...
Long story short the stone was a UFO that took me to Asgard
where Odin let me drink from the well
and I gave him my soul as barter.

In the Pig Pen

Bird of prey
hear what I say,
the hour has just begun
slaughter under the sun.

I play to feel the energy
the world's grace flows through my fingers.
Sounds becomes colors
inverting perception
of our self conscious minds.

Save us from eternal damnation,
may hellfire and brimstone be swept aside
unless we can not see the light.
Our mother waits for us on the wharf,
hell's boat eagerly bides until we are ready.

Killing daily
the king's men.
Lock away
in the pig pen
all of your evil emotion.

The Blues Saloon

Two men on horseback
ride in to town.
Darkness looms over
their large sun hats.
Thirsty
from spending weeks in the desert,
they head straight for the saloon.
Down the long empty street,
the only sound that can be herd
is sweat dripping from a brow.
Their destination was a
primeval cave
etched into a mountain side.
The sign above the door read,
Go Home.
What a fine establishment this looks like,
said the younger beardless man.
After tying up the horses,
the men moseyed on inside.
Drenched in the sound of blues piano
the air was heavy.
Sitting at the bar
alone
sat a man
with
a black
mac.
Good day said the younger beardless man.
Only a friendly nod was received
from the man in the black mac.
Do you like gin?
Said the older man with a long white beard.
Why certainly,

replied the man in the black mac,
take a seat
and I'll tell you a story.
Two men rode into town from the desert.
One much wiser than the other.
Do you know this story?
No but go on
says the younger beardless man.
Riding into town
they came across a lonesome fellow,
with experience beyond his days.
The younger of the two said,
good day sir,
we don't want any trouble in this town
we're just travelers from the far east.
Finally,
glancing up past his black travelers hat
the man pulled out a ivory six shooter
and shot the young man dead.
The older man said nothing
got off his horse
and closed the young mans eyes.
The older man turned to the lonesome fellow and said
do you like gin?
Why yes
replied the traveler
with a new found grin on his face,
and off they went to the blues saloon
on a day when all time was high noon.

Cambodia

You know we have no end
no beginning
only a middle
where we dance in the moonlight
praising the beat of the drum
Fall my sweet child
cry as we all die in the sunrise
waiting to be reborn as the moon takes the throne
dance
dance
lose all ability to feel your body
float freely through the soft night air
grow out your hair
be natural
lose your beautiful creations
they block out a pathway to the heavens
Cambodia

I Was a Fool Made Wise

I came home one morning
to check on my old lady,
but to my surprise
I was a fool made wise.

There was another man
oh lord there was another man,
you know I wanted to shoot'em both.
Down to the ground
yeah the blood would be all around.

But I'm leaving this place,
I'm done with this race.
I pulled out my gun
and they started to run.

A body fell with a smack
that was the end of that.

I hope you understand my story
even though it didn't end in glory.
A man died but his soul survived.
His mind had been revived.

I came home one morning
to check on my old lady,
but to my surprise
I was a fool made wise.

Today I sit with the gods
we rejoice in Valhalla.
My baby's evil deed
was one of greed,

I ride a lion hearted steed
through the gates of Avalon.

Those angels knew my love
she's not worthy of a dove,
in the skies up above
we dance merely.

Our Invitation

You see that over the horizon,
they're calling us to join them,
run rampant through the streets
a spell has been cast on our feet.

The gods of yester year
sit in the heavenly hall drinking beer,
our invitation can be complete
when we storm the kings castle.

His troops are ready for battle
they stand at guard at the door,
death floats above the impending battle ground
and the villagers prepare the burial mounds.

Are you ready for this final fight
this will be our final chance at everlasting light,
I hope the gods are on our side
so we can rejoice in Valhalla, oh heavenly castle.

In the End

We wait for the lighting
we wait for the hell fire,
hammer of the gods
will light the funeral pyre.

In the distance
darkness covers the sky,
but for now
the sun rides up high.

Typhoon
monsoon
the rains are coming
impending doom.

Read the great book
hear about the gore,
just wait
they're will be more.
Oh hell yes
the gods bring more
they're knocking on your door.

The villagers flee
the king rings the bell,
wolves run into town
thinking its a feast from hell.

Send out the call
warriors from the caves
they can save us all
strong hearts make them brave.

The Black Arrow

Poetry is in battle
hear our swords rattle.
We wait for the hour
Othin strikes us with power,
hammer of Thor falls
Ygg sends us a call.
It's time to travel across the Bilröst
only our life it will cost.

Ascending into Asgard
we fly like the black arrow of Bard.
Shades never made
dance in the sky,
in the distance
I can see Valhalla
if I try
and don't lie.

Courage brought me here
never was there any fear.
A smile on my face
as he hit me with a mace,
for I knew
I would be in the sky
true
as the black arrow flew.

The Internet is a Religion

The internet is a religion
bent on total mind control.
It draws you in with an amplified version
of a previous deception.
You are all pigs in this endless game of secret mind control,
and who created this game?
We did.

Alone in the forest we wandered for seven days,
searching for someone to hold us.
Endlessly we came across a being
that defied all others.

He wanted to lead us away from the cave,
but instead of listening
we stayed.
forever destined to destroy one another
instead of help one another.

Carelessly he left the crowd
smiling
he took hold of the staff
with a laugh saying,
I will serve forever
in the divine presence of glory.

Eternities pass and finally our hero is risen.
The dark age of hysterical
blood-shed
and tears,
can finally be swept away with one word.
Peace.

Victory in Valhalla

Standing over the canyon
he was waiting for a sign,
thinking about the stars
wondering why people whine.

Until the yellow one descended
with a blackened aura it transcended,
landing on his vest it said,
why do you rest?

Take life
our beautiful existence,
and run with it.
You are only alive when you try.

Waiting for it to lead you is good
but you need to search,
ramble through the forest.
It will find you
true as the sky is blue.

Without a doubt
it will remove that pout, and
whisper into you ear
the answer of your question
in other tongues, yet spoken clear.

Now take your lesson
travel to all the towns,
tell the one with the crown
to remove that awful frown.

Lead them back into the forest
back into their home,
join the mother
rejoice with the father.
Love your brother
be one and another
no different from any other.

Find the castle
hidden near the brook.
Beside mammoth willows
is where the brook will begin.

They caress the water
with the slightest breeze,
bending existence with ease.

These mighty trees
are the ones to please,
surviving all
they never fall.
The right kings of the castle,
I hope you find them with little hassle.

Around the bend
of this mighty river,
the trees send
news of the trend.

The villagers are coming,
marching towards to the hillside.
Dancing in the moonlight,
with Mother Earth they ride.

Over the crest
our hero sails,
he is without rest
on an unmarked trail.

The last thing on his mind
is what he will find
at the end his quest
one to save those who rest.

Surrounding him
trees of all colors,
scotch red
camouflage fed
pine bed
watch where you tread.

Signs of an epic journey
stretch across the sky,
flashes of victory fly by.

Entering the valley
no foe stood before him,
they were all at the bar drinking gin.

www.ingramcontent.com/pod-product-compliance
Lightning Source LLC
Chambersburg PA
CBHW032036040426
42449CB00007B/902